Destined by God

Barbara Shaw

Palmer Enterprises

Reflecting the Light of God's Word

Destined by God

ISBN: 978-0-9913483-6-7

Published by Palmer Enterprises
1971 Ellsworth Drive
Lakeside Marblehead, OH 43440 USA
Email: palmer2916@roadrunner.com

All Scripture quotations are taken from the King James Version of the Bible.

Some of the names of the people portrayed in this book have been changed to respect their privacy.

CONTENTS

Acknowledgments

For the development of this book, I feel a deep sense of gratitude to:

My parents, who taught me that the most wonderful and important relationship that I could ever have is with Jesus Christ.

My precious children, April and Renee, for their love, patience, and understanding over the years. You make it easy to fulfill God's will.

Kathy Palmer, my lifetime friend, who transcribed, advised, and labored with me to bring this book to life. Your ability to capture the essence of my heart and mind is a work of excellence.

Introduction

This is my testimony of the love of the Lord Jesus Christ and the power of His anointing. God has equipped me with power to overcome many obstacles. Even when I didn't "feel" His presence, God accomplished amazing things in my life, and He is not finished with me, yet.

I have learned through the years that without God we are nothing. He loved me when I was unlovable, because He *is* love. I am so grateful that He lives in me every moment of every day. I am constantly blown away by His powerful love. No matter what we go through, God can use it for His glory and as a testament of His power to change a life.

According to Dictionary.com[1], "destined" is defined: "1) bound for a certain destination: 2) ordained, appointed, or predetermined to be or do something." I am certainly bound for the destination God has for me!

I am not ashamed of the Gospel of Jesus Christ: for it is the power of God unto salvation. (Romans 1:16)

---

[1] http://www.dictionary.com/browse/destined

Chapter One
My Early Years

I was born in 1949 to Charles and Agnes Smith and grew up in LaBelle, a small coal mining town in southwestern Pennsylvania, which is located about 50 miles south of Pittsburgh. My parents received Jesus Christ as Savior when I was very young, so I was blessed to be raised in a Christian home.

My parents loved the Lord with all their hearts and were committed to raising my two brothers and I in the admonition of the Lord.

Train up a child in the way he should go: and when he is old, he will not depart from it.

(Proverbs 22:6)

My grandmother and great grandmother lived across the street from us, and they were Christians as well. My grandfather built the small church we attended, and he was also the pastor. My brothers and I went to Sunday School and church every Sunday.

My great grandmother believed in God, but my great grandfather was not a Christian. Because he did not follow Christ, he treated my great grandmother very poorly and was verbally abusive to her, often cursing at her for no reason. My great grandmother loved God with all her heart, despite the abuse she endured from her husband.

The Fear of the Lord

Even though I was blessed with a Christian heritage, my grandparents portrayed God in a way that made me fear Him. I feared Him so much that there was no room in my heart to love and trust Him. I reverenced God, but I feared Him more than anything else.

The image I had of God was as a strict disciplinarian waiting for me to sin, so He could punish me. From what I was taught, I thought

He was mean, and He didn't want anyone to have fun. Of course, many years later, I learned that was not true. The truth is God

> GOD IS
> LOVE IN
> ITS PUREST
> FORM

is love in its purest form. Without God, we cannot know what true love is. His tender love, compassion, and mercy springs forth renewed <u>every</u> morning.

> *It is of the LORD's mercies that we are not*
> *consumed, because his compassions fail*
> *not. They are new every morning: great*
> *is thy faithfulness.*
> *(Lamentations 3:22-23)*

The "fear of the Lord" that God wants us to have is an awe and reverence that draws us closer to Him, not fear that drives us away. This awe-inspiring reverence is like the breathtaking splendor of seeing the ocean for the first time. It's the awe felt when standing on the edge of the Grand Canyon or observing satellite images of God's infinite universe.

The fear of the LORD is the beginning of wisdom...   (Proverbs 9:10a)

If thou seekest her as silver, and searchest for her as for hid treasures; then shalt thou understand the fear of the LORD, and find the knowledge of God.   (Proverbs 2:4-5)

The fear and awe of the Lord that God desires you to have will always draw you closer to Him, not drive you away.

A Christian Heritage

My brothers and I grew up in church. At that time, church was boring to me. I could not comprehend much of what I heard and witnessed. Many of the people I saw in church, including the preachers, were doing things they were telling us not to do. As a young child, this was very confusing, and I didn't know what to believe. I was unaware that I could know God personally and have an intimate, glorious relationship with Him.

The LORD hath appeared of old unto me, saying, Yea, I have loved thee with an everlasting love: therefore with loving-kindness have I drawn thee.

(Jeremiah 31:3)

As an adult, I now realize that we, as Christians, are God's masterpiece, and we must exhibit lives that are holy, separated, sanctified to Him. Our family, friends, coworkers, and neighbors are watching us and reading our lives.

Ye are our epistle written in our hearts, known and read of all men: Forasmuch as ye are manifestly declared to be the epistle of Christ ministered by us, written not with ink, but with the Spirit of the living God; not in tables of stone, but in fleshly tables of the heart.

(2 Corinthians 3:2-3)

We are living epistles (letters) from the Lord. We must be constantly aware of what our lives are saying to others about Jesus Christ when they observe us.

A Wholesome Life

My dad was a coal miner and worked hard so that we could live a nice, comfortable life. Yes, I was a coal miner's daughter. Since I was the only girl, my dad treated me like a princess. I felt so much love and protection from my mom and dad. We were not rich, but my brothers and I had all that we needed. We were so blessed. We had a nice home, and God blessed us with more than most. We knew without a doubt that we were loved.

I had a wonderful upbringing and had everything as a child. My mom and dad took us on church picnics, and we went on family vacations every summer. We had so much fun.

Some vacations were spent with my Aunt Fran and Uncle Bill in Cleveland, Ohio, which I thoroughly enjoyed. It was exciting, because we were in the big city and met a lot of kids.

My Aunt Fran and Uncle Bill had five kids (four daughters and a son). My Aunt Fran gave birth to her son, Carl, out of wedlock, when she was young, and so Carl was raised by my grandmother, Aunt Fran's mother, who lived across the street from us.

Carl always seemed different from the other kids. He was tormented by dreams of death and snakes. We did not realize, at the time, that our great grandfather was sexually abusing him. Sadly, Carl was tormented all his life and died in his early 40s. I'll discuss the cause of Carl's death in Chapter 4.

The Call of the City

I graduated high school and longed to live in the city. My desire to pursue a career in the city grew from those visits to Cleveland when I was young. I did not realize God was dealing with me even then. God was

> THE SEED WAS PLANTED

planting a seed within me that came to fruition as I matured.

In high school I got engaged, but broke it off. I realized I wanted a career in New York City and felt destined for something greater.

For the vision is yet for an appointed time, but at the end it shall speak, and not lie: though it tarry, wait for it;

because it will surely come, it will not tarry.

(Habakkuk 2:3)

My parents were adamant that I was not going to go all the way to New York. We compromised, and I moved to Pittsburgh. I worked there for a short period, but didn't like it and moved back home.

At 19, I was still a virgin. My mother taught me God's Word and how it applied to Christian integrity and purity for women. I accepted this teaching wholeheartedly and did not allow a boy to touch me in a carnal way.

For this is the will of God, even your sanctification, that ye should abstain from fornication.

(1 Thessalonians 4:3-5)

After returning from Pittsburgh, I grew more and more discontented in LaBelle. There were no jobs; I was bored and restless. I wanted to leave desperately, but didn't know where to go.

As a young woman with nothing to occupy my time, I began having sexual desires. An idle mind truly is the devil's playground. My boyfriend at the time began pressuring me to have sex; and I knew that if I stayed in LaBelle with nothing to do, I would eventually give in.

I told my mom how I felt, and she talked it over with my dad. They called my uncle and aunt in Brooklyn, New York. My uncle and aunt agreed it would be best for me to live with them for a while, and my mother and grandmother rode with me on the bus to New York City.

Chapter Two
New York, New York!

I was only in New York City for two weeks when I secured a position with the New York Telephone Company on Broad Street near South Ferry. It was very exciting. I worked with data processing in the Switching Control Center.

Well, what can I say about New York? It was so exciting to see the skyscrapers, meet people from all over the world, and see the United Nations buildings. I also worked on Wall Street and in the World Trade Center.

I loved my job very much, and I loved the people I worked with. My boss was Richard Schroeder, whose son is the famous actor, Ricky Schroeder. When Ricky was a little boy, his father would bring him to the office, and I would babysit him while his dad was in meetings.

The Dating Scene

There were so many attractive men working within the telephone company. So, naturally, I started dating. I met Paul, who was much older, and began having sex for the first time at 21 years of age. If only I knew then what I know now, I would have listened to God when He said no sex before marriage. Oh, how I wish I'd had a personal relationship with Jesus Christ. I would have saved myself a lot of pain and sorrow.

HINDSIGHT IS 20/20

I have discovered that God's way is the best way, the only way, the perfect way. After all, Jesus is the way, the truth, and the life.

Jesus saith unto him, I am the way, the truth, and the life: no man cometh unto the Father, but by me.

(John 14:6)

I thought I was in love with Paul. Although he was married, I justified in my mind that it was okay because he and his wife had been separated for many years. They just never got a divorce. Of course, in God's eyes, it was wrong no matter how I tried to rationalize it.

In the natural progression of my sin, Paul introduced me to alcohol. Now, I was sliding further and further into darkness: dating a married man, getting drunk, and having sex.

The Broad Path

Enter ye in at the strait gate: for wide is the gate, and broad is the way, that leadeth to destruction, and many there be which go in thereat: Because strait is the gate, and narrow is the way, which leadeth unto life, and few there be that find it.

(Matthew 7:13-14)

At 22 years of age, I loved the nightlife of New York, going to bars with Paul and attending parties. It was so much fun that I stayed out all night on occasion. When I came home to where

I lived with my aunt and uncle, we got into bitter arguments. Since I worked hard and gave them money for rent, I thought I could do whatever I wanted. Of course, I was wrong, and I was being very disrespectful.

As I got to know Paul, I found out that he and I were from the same town. I didn't know him when I was growing up, however, because he was much older than me. I attended the same school as his brothers and sisters.

Though Paul drank a lot of beer and smoked a lot, he treated me very well and was never abusive. Even though he did anything I wanted him to do, the relationship was still destructive, because I was going against all of the sound and godly principles I had been taught.

I knew there was a God, but I did not want to serve Him. I just wanted to have fun. I figured I'd serve Him later, after I got older. What a mistake that was. God's way is truly the only way to live an abundant life.

The thief cometh not, but for to steal, and to kill, and to destroy: I am come that they might have life, and that they might have it more abundantly.

(John 10:10)

Utter Chaos

Life with my uncle and aunt in Brooklyn was chaotic. My Uncle Steve was a drunk; and though he treated my Aunt Shirley badly, she remained loyal to him. She stuck by him even after he got my aunt's best friend pregnant.

Uncle Steve would come home drunk late at night and make everyone in the house get out of bed and listen to him rant and rave. We never even understood what he was talking about.

For God is not the author of confusion, but of peace...

(1 Corinthians 14:33a)

Because of Uncle Steve's abusive behavior, I did not respect him.

One bright spot in this chaotic household was my cousin, who came from South Carolina to live with us. She was Uncle Steve's daughter from his first marriage. Though she was much younger than me, we got along very well.

An Innocent Life Cut Short

I was still running around with Paul and found out I was pregnant. To make matters worse, of course, he did not want a baby. So, I went to get a legal and "safe" abortion. Back then, I bought into the widespread lie that an abortion was certainly a perfectly acceptable form of birth control and an acceptable medical procedure. There was nothing wrong with that. After all, it was just a fetus, not a baby. I was so very wrong. Again, in my mind, I was justifying my sinful behavior.

> I KEPT JUSTIFYING MY SIN

God proclaims in His Word that He knew us from the foundation of the world.

> *According as he hath chosen us in him before the foundation of the world, that we should be holy and without blame before him in love.* (Ephesians 1:4)

He knew me before I was conceived in my mother's womb.

Before I formed thee in the belly I knew thee; and before thou camest forth out of the womb I sanctified thee, and I ordained thee a prophet unto the nations.   (Jeremiah 1:5)

I didn't understand at the time that I was killing my baby. I paid for my baby to be murdered. I now know the horrifying truth: I was enriching others at the cost of my baby's life.

There were many women at the abortion mill. It was such a sad and scary time, because we were all there having our babies killed. In reality, we were like a herd of cattle leading our own babies to the slaughter. We were having our babies slaughtered for profit. Without God, we are such fools.

I hid the abortion from my aunt and uncle. They never found out; however, the Word of God warns that we will reap what we sow.

Be not deceived; God is not mocked: for whatsoever a man soweth, that shall he also reap.   (Galatians 6:7)

Be careful what you do, for your sin will find you out.

But if ye will not do so, behold, ye have sinned against the LORD: and be sure your sin will find you out.

(Numbers 32:23)

I observed all the young girls and women in a big room, writhing in excruciating pain after having their abortions. We were lying in beds that were covered with blood-soaked sheets, the brutal aftermath of having our babies ripped from our wombs.

There were just as many in the hallway waiting to go through the same horrific experience. What an awful, nightmarish sight! Without God, we make all the wrong choices.

The Consequences of Sin

After the abortion, I went home and noticed I was still bleeding very heavily. I was horrified to see big clots of blood flowing out of me, and I was in terrible pain. I went back to the doctor, and I was prescribed medication to stop the bleeding, and the bleeding finally stopped.

I did not realize the instruments they used to perform the abortion were not sterilized. Because of this, now my appendix was infected and had ruptured, but no one knew. I was extremely sick, and

> **THIS NIGHTMARE WAS FAR FROM OVER**

my temperature was very high. I couldn't lay down and sleep, because I couldn't breathe if I did.

My aunt took me to the emergency room, where the doctor examined me and told me I had an ulcer and to go home and take Tylenol for pain. I kept getting worse; unbeknownst to me, my appendix ruptured Thanksgiving Day.

My mother came from Pennsylvania to take me home, because nothing was being done for me in New York. The doctor did not even detect that my appendix had ruptured. Once I arrived home, I seemed to feel better.

It didn't last, though, and I started getting sick again. My mom took me to another doctor. My ruptured appendix still wasn't detected. The doctor gave me medication, and my mom took me back home. For a while, it seemed I was doing okay. I even felt well enough to go shopping with my mom.

During this time, my brothers were still living at home. My older brother was there with his wife, and they had the bedroom next to mine. My younger brother and I shared a room, where there were two single beds.

After falling asleep one night, I became very ill. My younger brother called for my mom, and they rushed me to the hospital. After the doctor examined me, he told my mom he would have to do exploratory surgery so that he could look inside and find the cause of my high fever and pain.

Ultrasound equipment had not yet been invented. There were no machines that could provide an x-ray of internal organs; therefore, I had to have my stomach cut open.

After they looked inside, they sewed me up and told my parents there was nothing they could do, because poison and bruised blood had infected my entire body inside. As I mentioned earlier, my appendix ruptured Thanksgiving Day; the exploratory surgery was not performed until Christmas Eve. I had been walking around all that time with that poison in my body.

God is so merciful and loving. Even though the pain and anguish I was experiencing was due to my own sin, He sustained me. Even though I was not seeking Him, He sought me.

God was with me, and I had a call on my life. God declared I would live and not die, so that I could declare His mighty works.

> *I shall not die, but live, and declare the works of the LORD.*
>
> *(Psalm 118:17)*

When the doctor announced to my parents there was nothing he could do, my mom began crying. The doctor looked at her and told her he would try everything he could to save my life.

I was admitted to the hospital in critical condition. There were tubes running down my nose to my stomach and out of my stomach, hooked up to a machine pumping poison out of my body. There were also tubes in my arms where medicine flowed to my veins constantly. I was in for the battle of my life.

I could not eat, so they had to feed me through my veins. My temperature was so high that they had to keep me on a water bed to try to keep my ever-soaring temperature down to a safe level. Even now, I can vividly remember the day my older brother came to the hospital to see me. I looked so bad that he rushed out of the room crying, because he could not stand to see me in such agony.

GOD DID NOT ABANDON ME

Because of the poison throughout my body, my body started to emit a putrid odor. I lost so much weight that I looked like I was starving to death, like someone you see on television from a third world country who is malnourished. It was a very painful time in my life, but God was with me.

> *... for he hath said, I will never leave thee, nor forsake thee.*
>
> *(Hebrews 13:5b)*

One night, I was given a blood transfusion. I was told, later, that the blood they gave me was infected with alcohol, so I kept hallucinating and thought the nurses were trying to hurt me. I was so delirious, I had to be strapped down.

My arms were stuck so many times to inject pain medication that there were tracks down both arms from the needles, and my arms were black and blue from the injections. My temperature reached 103-104, and I had tubes running everywhere, and I also had a catheter.

I told my mom to send for my great grandmother. My great grandmother had been a Christian for as long as I could remember; and when she prayed, things happened. I knew if she would come and pray, that God would answer, and I would be healed. I needed a radical prayer partner, someone to stand in agreement with me in absolute faith that God would heal me.

God promises in His Word that where two or three are gathered in His name, there He will be in the midst, and He will hear and answer our prayers!

> *Again I say unto you, That if two of you shall agree on earth as touching any thing that they shall ask, it shall be done for them of my Father which is in heaven. For where two or three are gathered together in my name, there am I in the midst of them.*
>
> *(Matthew 18:19-20)*

A Phenomenal Healing

My great grandmother was brought to the hospital. She looked into my eyes and started praying. As she prayed, I heard God say, "Touch the hem of her coat," which became a point of contact for my miracle.

God reminded me of His Word, the Bible, about the story of the woman with the issue of blood, how that woman made her way through

the crowd to touch the hem of Jesus' garment.
Her faith, touching Jesus, made her whole.

> *And, behold, a woman, which was
> diseased with an issue of blood twelve
> years, came behind him, and touched the
> hem of his garment: For she said within
> herself, If I may but touch his garment, I
> shall be whole. But Jesus turned him
> about, and when he saw her, he said,
> Daughter, be of good comfort; thy faith
> hath made thee whole. And the woman
> was made whole from that hour.*
>
> *(Matthew 9:20-22)*

It is a good thing to be saturated in the Word
of God, because in your worst times, you can
draw from its pages and be healed, delivered,
and set free! God's Word is true, and His Word
gives us victory!

> *He sent his word, and healed them, and
> delivered them from their destructions.*
>
> *(Psalm 107:20)*

During the time I was lying in the hospital, I sensed God's presence and felt He was talking to me. I knew that I had to touch the hem of my great grandmother's coat while she was praying. As she was leaving the hospital, before she could even exit the building, I started feeling very hot.

My dad was sitting in the chair by my bed, where he sat every night, while my mom was home with my brothers. I heard God say, "Sit up." You have to understand that I could not sit up on my own. I was hooked up to IVs and a machine pumping poison out of my body, with tubes everywhere.

I sat up, and my father was stunned. He did not know what I was trying to do. God then said,

STAND UP!

"Stand up!" I had not been able to stand, because my legs were so weak. I stood up, and my father grew fearful. He called the nurse and then asked me what I was trying to do. All I knew was that I had to get up out of that bed!

When I stood up, an abscess on my stomach ruptured and all the poison, bruised blood, and pus that the machine couldn't pump out, came running out. It was awesome! God performed a miracle that I will never forget!

I went home two weeks after that. I had been in the hospital a total of one and a half months. The hospital staff was amazed, because they did not think I was going to make it.

God is so faithful! I had a call on my life, although I didn't know it. I was destined by God for more than I could even think or imagine.

> *Now unto him that is able to do exceeding abundantly above all that we ask or think, according to the power that worketh in us, unto him be glory in the church by Christ Jesus throughout all ages, world without end. Amen.*
>
> *(Ephesians 3:20-21)*

During my last two weeks in the hospital, I had to have therapy to strengthen my legs, so that I could walk. My stomach had to be trained to receive and hold solid food, because I had been fed with an IV for several weeks.

As I was leaving the hospital, I thanked my doctor, Dr. Carpenter, for all he had done. I'll never forget him. He told me to thank God, not him, because he hadn't known what to do. He said they were just experimenting with me. He declared he had never heard of anyone walking around with a ruptured appendix as long as I had and then live to tell about it.

I went home with my parents and stayed with them until the doctor said I was well enough to travel back to New York to work. After six months in Pennsylvania, I was eager to get back to New York City.

The Triumphant Return

When I went back to work, everyone was glad to see me. I had been out of the office on disability for one year, and the telephone company owed me a large sum of money. So not only did God heal me, He provided me with a huge financial blessing.

God turned what Satan intended for evil into something good.

> *But as for you, ye thought evil against me; but God meant it unto good, to bring to pass, as it is this day, to save much people alive.*   (Genesis 50:20)

God works all things together for good to those who love Him.

> *And we know that all things work together for good to them that love God, to them who are the called according to his purpose.*
>
> (Romans 8:28)

Slipping into Darkness

After the trauma my body had been through, I suffered emotional problems and became very hypersensitive. I seemed to always be annoyed, even at minor things, and I kept arguing with my aunt and uncle, who had let me move back in with them. I refused **SOMETHING WAS TERRIBLY WRONG** to clean my room or even make my bed. I had totally changed, and my aunt and uncle knew something was terribly wrong.

Eventually, I moved out of my aunt and uncle's home and moved in with my boyfriend, Paul. I was not thinking about God. I soon forgot what He had done for me. I just wanted to "do my own thing," which was a huge mistake. I stayed with Paul for a couple of years, and all we did was drink and go to a lot of parties and bars.

God was still protecting me and guarding the destiny He had for me, even as I again turned my back on Him and went my own way, not serving Him, not accepting Him as the Lord of my life.

> *For I know the thoughts that I think toward you, saith the LORD, thoughts of peace, and not of evil, to give you an expected end.*
>
> *(Jeremiah 29:11)*

One day, I met a man on the job named Dan. We started going out to some of the New York night spots, partying, drinking, and staying out all night, even though I was still living with Paul.

One evening, while Dan and I were out on a date, Dan asked me to marry him. I was impressed by his status as the star basketball player for the New York Telephone Company, and I said yes.

I went back to Paul's, got my belongings, and moved in with Dan in Patterson, New Jersey. After a couple of months, he decided he didn't want to be married any longer, so he started staying out and coming home drunk. We finally ended the marriage.

I was devastated. I just wanted to be married and have a family. I had been taught that, at a certain age, you got married and stayed married, so divorce was very painful for me.

I ended up getting my own apartment in Brooklyn. By this time, I was about 25 years old. I started dating different men; I always had a boyfriend. I had a good job with the telephone company, and money was no problem, so I thought I had it made.

Even though I was raised in a Christian home, I did not have a personal relationship with God through Jesus Christ, so everything I could do, I did. New York City was a very exciting place to live and work. I loved the Broadway shows. I even walked the streets with movie stars and watched them make movies on the city streets.

New York City is a melting pot where many ethnic groups live and raise their families. While I worked at the telephone company, I met people from all over the world, from various cultures and ethnic backgrounds.

I loved going to Chinatown. They had the best Chinese food ever. Little Italy made me feel like I was in Europe.

Although I liked almost everything about New York City, I didn't like the subway, because there were many unstable people riding on the subway.

A Close Call

While I was at work, one day, someone broke into my apartment. They came in through a window and stole my television. I stayed home the next day, in case they came back, to see if I could catch who did it.

I was awakened by a noise at the door early in the morning. I got up and quietly made my way to the door and looked out the peep hole. I saw a man trying to pick the lock on my door, so that he could gain access to my apartment. I was terrified!

I ran to the phone and instead of dialing 911, I frantically called my mother in Pennsylvania. She told me to hang up and call the police. I was so nervous that I could not dial 911. I called my job, and they contacted the police. When the police arrived, I pointed the man out. The man was so bold that he had not even left the area. He was standing right in front of my building!

CALL 911!

I found out later that he had just recently been released from prison, where he had served time for murdering someone. I had to go to court and testify against this man, a convicted murderer, before he could be convicted yet again for another crime and returned to prison.

I ended up putting my furniture in storage and moving back in with my aunt and uncle. I was glad to be with them and felt protected. This time, I respected their home and appreciated them. I gave them absolutely no trouble.

Chapter Three

Disastrous Decisions

While on my way to work one day, a man named Tyrone started flirting with me. He was very attractive, and we struck up a conversation. After we dated a while, I found out that he was married with two small children. That didn't dissuade me from continuing the relationship. His wife had left him, so I justified in my mind that it was okay to continue seeing him. It proved to be a very bad decision.

Tyrone's wife returned home, but still our relationship persisted. His wife left again for good, and I moved in with him. What a tragic blunder! If only I had submitted my life to God, He would have saved me from the evil I was about to embrace.

Submit yourselves therefore to God. Resist the devil, and he will flee from you.

(James 4:7)

Tyrone's wife filed for divorce, and I wanted to marry him, which was yet another very bad decision. When we do not follow God and get to know Him and His ways, we are fools and do not discern danger. God's way is the only way. Living a life of sin and embracing Satan's ways will only lead to death and destruction. Satan's total purpose and design for anyone's life is to steal, kill, and destroy God's destiny for them.

But once again, what Satan meant for evil, God turned around for good and blessed me with two very beautiful daughters who are saved, sanctified, and filled with the amazing Holy Spirit! Praise God! When you turn to God, He will save and deliver you!

GOD CAN TURN IT AROUND

I Was Forewarned

Before Tyrone's divorce was final, his wife called me and told me how abusive he was. His wife and his wife's mother begged me not to marry Tyrone and pleaded with me to leave him. They tried their best to save me from the pain that they warned was sure to come, but I would not listen.

I did not believe his wife. I thought I was a better woman than she was and that he would not treat me the way he had treated her. After all, she must have done something wrong for Tyrone to abuse her. Boy, was I ever wrong.

When Tyrone's wife left him, she left him with an apartment full of furniture. I remember making a statement to a friend of mine that I thought she was stupid for leaving him with everything. I let my friend know that if I would ever have to leave, I certainly wouldn't do something as dumb as that.

Be careful of the words that you speak. Later, I had to leave Tyrone, and I left behind a house full of furniture, my car, and my career.

Chapter Four
Married Life

Well, Tyrone and I finally got married. We went back to my hometown for the wedding. It was very nice. My parents were very happy. My brothers did not like my future husband; but because I wanted to marry him, they went along with it.

After two weeks, we went back to Staten Island, New York. The apartment complex we lived in was called Parkhill. A couple of weeks after we moved in, I discovered that many of those living around us were doing drugs.

Tyrone and I both worked for the telephone company and had very good incomes, so I told him that I wanted to move. We found a beautiful garden apartment in a complex that had a pool, and we moved in.

Tyrone introduced me to marijuana (pot), and I liked it. When we weren't working, all we did was party. I became a pothead and an alcoholic. I also sniffed cocaine and embalming fluid. How tragic!

Because I only got high after work, nobody knew, because I still went to work every day. Most of our friends got high like we did. I had a lot of fun until the realization hit me that I was addicted and could not stop. Suddenly I came to know real bondage, and there seemed to be no way to escape the snare of the enemy.

Saved!

While going about my daily routine one day, I heard God plainly say, "Barbara, it's time." Somehow I knew what He meant. I told a friend of mine that I had to give my life to God, and she said that she also wanted to give her life to Him.

We located a Spirit-filled church on Staten Island and went together one Sunday morning. When they gave the altar call on that marvelous day, I ran to the front of the church and surrendered my life to Jesus!

When I stopped going to parties with my husband and told him that I was saved, that's when all hell broke loose! Physical, emotional, and even horrible sexual abuse began. Soon Tyrone began running wild and living a dark, adulterous lifestyle. He would punch me, even when I was pregnant with our first daughter. He would kick me, try to throw me out of bed, and tried to throw me down the stairs.

> HELL ON EARTH!

Tyrone grew insane, constantly arguing, and cursing, and threatening my life. It was like hell here on earth. The more he abused me, the more I drank and got high. I was living a nightmare. What I was experiencing just could not be happening. Tyrone acted worse than an animal.

A Generational Curse

I began to notice that Tyrone's father treated Tyrone's mother the same way. Without God, we have no clue of how to treat those we say we love and have vowed to honor and protect. Tyrone's father never had anything good to say about or to Tyrone's mother.

Tyrone's father was diagnosed with stomach cancer, and we went to see him almost daily. Tyrone's father was always kind to me, even though he was mean to his wife. I noticed that Tyrone's parents never hugged any of their children, never encouraged them, and never spoke positive words over them.

Tyrone's father was always arguing with Tyrone's mother about something. Most of the time, she didn't know what he was complaining about. She could never please him, no matter what she said or did. Tyrone's only role model was his father, and Tyrone embraced that generational curse with a vengeance.

Tyrone's brother was one year younger than him and was a drug addict. Tyrone had two stepsisters that were older than him. His youngest sister, Kathy, was married with three kids and lived in Brooklyn.

My husband was very insecure. Because he was unfaithful to me, he always accused me of being unfaithful. I was trapped in a horrifying life of bondage and abuse. I cried out to God daily to deliver me from the hand of the wicked.

And the L ORD shall help them, and deliver them: he shall deliver them from the wicked, and save them, because they trust in him.

(Psalm 37:40)

The American Dream

Despite our rocky marriage, Tyrone and I bought a house on Norwood Avenue in Staten Island. The neighborhood was very nice, and we had wonderful neighbors. I could look down the street and see a very stunning view of the Statue of Liberty. It was a beautiful sight to see all the boats

WHATEVER WE WANTED, WE BOUGHT.

coming in and out of New York Harbor. Outwardly, we seemed to be living the American dream. We each had our own car. Money was no problem. Whatever we wanted, we bought.

Everyone thought I had the perfect marriage and family. We had two beautiful daughters, and my oldest daughter went to Catholic school. No one knew I was being abused almost daily.

I did everything I could to please Tyrone; no matter how hard I tried, he found fault with me. I was so miserable and depressed. I started going to a psychologist, who was very helpful.

Tyrone would sometimes dream that I was with someone else and would then awaken and beat me because of his dream. The police were at my house on a weekly basis. A policeman once told me that Tyrone was a very dangerous man and warned me that Tyrone may eventually try to kill me. I was afraid to leave, even though I knew that I had to get to a safe place.

Horrifying Betrayal

One day when I went to work, on a normal day like any other day, my supervisor divulged to me that she was having problems with her fiancé. She revealed that he was abusing her. Soon after she confided in me, she did not come to work for three days; and when she finally did come back, she told me her fiancé had tied her up so she could not leave the house.

She got an order of protection and moved from Long Island, where they were living, to Queens, New York, with her two sisters. She thought she was safe.

One evening, she was standing with her two sisters on a subway platform waiting for the train. She heard a click and turned around. Her fiancé was standing there with a double barreled shotgun. She turned to run, and he shot her in the back. Her heart was blown out of her chest, split in two, and laid there on the platform. She died instantly.

Her fiancé shot her two sisters, also, but they survived, even though one of her sister's arms was severely damaged. It was the biggest story reported by the news media at that time.

A House Is Not a Home

When I went home that day, I told my husband what happened, and his sinister reply paralyzed me with fear. He said, "If someone wants to kill you, an order of protection won't stop them." It frightened me, because he had already threatened to kill me.

I was married to this insane man, because I wanted to take what someone else had – or thought I did. But now I was reaping what I had sown, and it was very devastating to me and my children. I did not understand that when I chose this man to be my husband, I was also choosing the head of my house, the priest of my home, the provider of my household, and the father of my children.

Without God, we have no wisdom at all. A family's home should be the safest place for them. Unfortunately, many homes, today, as mine was, are very, very unsafe, dangerous places to be. I felt safer on the streets of New York City than I did in my own home. It was so terrifying, it makes me shudder to even think about it.

> YOUR HOME SHOULD BE A SAFE PLACE

I prayed daily for the situation to change. I fasted 14 days with just water. Although the congregation of the church I attended at the time prayed for my marriage, Tyrone grew worse. God would not go against Tyrone's own will. God wants us to come to Him willingly, not because someone else forces us to.

Fasting is meant to change the person who is fasting and not to be used as "voodoo" against someone else to get them to do what we want them to do; however, the change in the one fasting can affect a change in others because of the power, authority, and anointing of the Holy Spirit. Fasting increases your faith and helps you believe in miracles, and you will experience the power and glory of God!

> *Then he called for a light, and sprang in, and came trembling, and fell down before Paul and Silas, and brought them out, and said, Sirs, what must I do to be saved?*
>
> *(Acts 16:29-30)*

As I said before, if only I knew then what I know now! Although I was trying to follow God, I was so lost. I drank and smoked pot all the time, trying to escape the pain and sorrow. I worked every day, a mother of two, and Tyrone was beating me up at least once a week. I was going out of my mind – staying with my abuser, because I was afraid to leave. I was, in fact, paralyzed with fear; however, I knew that if I didn't get to a safe place, he would kill me.

Deliverance

On top of everything else I was going through with Tyrone, getting high and drinking became a serious problem for me. I cried out to God daily to deliver me from smoking pot. Satan had such a stronghold on my life in that area.

I called my mom, and I told her that I was addicted to pot and alcohol and that I was praying every day for deliverance. She told me that the fact that I wanted to quit was an indication that God was going to deliver me.

Sure enough, one day I was watching a show on television featuring David Toma.[2] He was an undercover cop in New York. He stated he had witnessed thousands of people whose lives had been destroyed by drugs. He further explained that marijuana kills brain cells.

---

[2] http://davidtoma.com/liffe-story/

God used that program to deliver me from drugs and alcohol many years ago. Praise God forever! I never had to go to a drug or alcohol treatment program.

God is so faithful. When we call out to Him, He hears and answers.

Tragedy Strikes

I got a call one day from my oldest brother saying that my younger brother had died of a heart attack due to mixing prescription drugs and alcohol. When I received that news, it hurt me so bad. I was devastated.

I was a baby Christian at that time, so my faith was very weak. During the funeral, I could not bear the hurt that I felt. My mom told me that the worst hurt for a parent is to outlive their child. My older brother took it worse than I did, because he and my younger brother were very close, almost inseparable.

My cousin Carl flew in from Germany. Since my grandmother had raised him and we lived across the street from each other as children and adolescents, Carl was more like a brother to me.

After the funeral, Carl disclosed that he had been sexually abused by our great grandfather. In addition to the devastation of my brother's sudden, untimely death, we were emotionally shattered by this horrific revelation by Carl.

We were so saddened that he had withstood such a nightmarish existence as a child. I now understood why God had put Carl so strongly on my heart over the years, leading me to pray for him constantly.

Pray without ceasing.
(1 Thessalonians 5:17)

Sadly, during the 1950s, when Carl went through this experience, children who were sexual abuse victims were ostracized and blamed for their abuse, as if it were their own fault. Because the culture at that time blamed the young victims, instead of the abusers, Carl was too ashamed and afraid to tell anyone what his great grandfather was doing to him. By the time Carl revealed his devastating secret to the family, our great grandfather had passed away years before.

Even though our great grandfather was not brought to justice by the legal system, he experienced an even worse punishment. Our great grandfather had horrible hallucinations as he lay dying. He kept screaming, "Help me! They're coming for me! The fire is too hot!" He had visions of hell as he lay dying; yet, he did not repent or call out to God for salvation.

Tragedy Strikes Again

I finally went back to New York, because I had to return to work. A year went by, and on Christmas Day I received a call from my brother telling me that my mom had an aneurysm and that she was in a coma.

I immediately felt an agonizing emotional pain that I cannot describe. I prayed. I cried out to God. I just knew that He would heal her and raise her up off of her bed of affliction.

Many are the afflictions of the righteous: but the LORD delivereth him out of them all.

(Psalm 34:19)

Even though I prayed for my mom to be healed, she passed away. I could not understand why she had to die. She was only 55 years old. How could she leave us? She loved God with all of her heart. Why would He allow this to happen?

I was reading my Bible, and He took me to the following verse:

Precious in the sight of the LORD is the death of his saints.

(Psalm 116:15)

The Holy Spirit comforted me through that time of indescribable grief. I know now that God's ways are not our ways.

For my thoughts are not your thoughts, neither are your ways my ways, saith the LORD. For as the heavens are higher than the earth, so are my ways higher than your ways, and my thoughts than your thoughts.

(Isaiah 55:8)

My mother's doctor informed me later that if she had lived, she would not have been able to do anything for herself or anyone else. She died peacefully in her sleep. She laid down to take a nap Christmas afternoon and woke up in the arms of Jesus. The doctor said she didn't feel any pain at all.

No matter what we go through, God is in control. Jesus is well aware of the sufferings we endure in this life, but He also knows the glory revealed in those who believe in and follow Him.

> GOD IS IN CONTROL!

For I reckon that the sufferings of this present time are not worthy to be compared with the glory which shall be revealed in us.

(Romans 8:18)

I was finally able to accept my mother's death. All she ever talked about was being with the Lord, and she was finally where she longed to be.

Time with My Dad

Tyrone and I got along for a while after my mother's death, and the abuse ceased for a season. But then he began to stay out all night and would come home and start arguing with me. Sadly, my first child was old enough to witness Tyrone abusing me and had to listen to his vulgar language.

Tyrone created such a tense environment. He constantly threatened me and would not even allow me to go home to visit what was left of my family. I felt such a strong call inside to go home that I could not sleep. I felt that I had to go visit my dad. Later, I realized it was God putting that strong desire within me to go home.

> A DESIRE
> TO GO
> HOME

Delight thyself also in the LORD: and he shall give thee the desires of thine heart.
(Psalm 37:4)

When my husband was at work one day, I took my one-year-old daughter, and we went to the airport and boarded a plane headed for Pennsylvania. <u>I had to go see my father</u>. It would be the first time he'd see his granddaughter.

When my husband discovered I was gone, he called my dad's house and cursed me and argued with my dad. My father was so upset. He begged me not to go back to New York, because he was very afraid for me. The next day, my husband turned up at my dad's front door. Reluctantly, I went back to New York.

When I went to work the next day, my boss called me into his office and told me that my dad was dead. I was so shocked! To this day, I believe that my dad had a heart attack because he was worried about me living with an extremely abusive husband.

I had to turn around and go back to Pennsylvania to bury my father. I remember his words to me the last time I saw him. He told me that he was so proud of me, because I had never given him any trouble. He also told me to remember that God is real, no matter what anyone else does or says. He told me to follow God and no one else.

Yet Another Family Tragedy

My brother moved his family into my parents' house. I went back to New York, and things were quiet for a while. After six years, I became pregnant again. I was sick inside.

I wanted to have an abortion. I tried to find every reason why I should not have another baby, but I could not escape the image of Jesus before me. The conviction was so great that I could not go through with the abortion.

I am so glad to have both of my daughters. They are my heart and a great blessing to me. I thank God for them.

One morning I received a phone call from my brother, and he told me that my cousin Carl was home from Germany, and he was very sick.

I packed up, and my daughters and I went to Pennsylvania to see my cousin. When I arrived, I discovered something that broke my heart and shattered it into a million pieces: my cousin had full-blown AIDS.

Carl had sores from head to toe. He had lost a lot of weight and looked so pitiful. He suffered horribly, and I will never forget it.

Because of the sexual abuse Carl suffered at the hands of my great grandfather, he felt drawn to the homosexual lifestyle; therefore, Carl would not acknowledge homosexuality as sin.

> *For this cause God gave them up unto vile affections: for even their women did change the natural use into that which is against nature: And likewise also the men, leaving the natural use of the woman, burned in their lust one toward another; men with men working that which is unseemly, and receiving in themselves that recompence of their error which was meet. And even as they did not like to retain God in their knowledge, God gave them over to a reprobate mind, to do those things which are not convenient...*
>
> *(Romans 1:26-28)*

Carl was raised in church, just as I was, and he knew the Word of God; but in the end Satan had him so bound and blind that he could not see the truth. Jesus promises the truth will make us free; however, we must first know the truth, and it is the truth that we know that makes us free.

TRUTH LIBERATES!

> *And ye shall know the truth, and the truth shall make you free.*
>
> *(John 8:32)*

Carl could not be set free, because he refused to acknowledge the truth. He stubbornly dug his heels in and just would not accept the Word of God.

I have heard some people say, "I'll wait until the last minute and accept Jesus Christ as my Savior." You may not have a chance in the last moments of your life to make that decision. My mother died in her sleep. Thankfully, she knew where she was going, because she had made that decision years earlier. Death could not rob her of her reward. She woke up in the arms of her Savior and Lord.

Carl's heart, however, had been hardened, and he just would not acknowledge the truth.

Wherefore (as the Holy Spirit saith, To day if ye will hear his voice, harden not your hearts, as in the provocation, in the day of temptation in the wilderness...) While it is said, To day if ye will hear his voice, harden not your hearts...
(Hebrews 3:7-8, 15)

Today is the day of salvation and tomorrow is promised to no one! Carl ran out of time. He grew worse and worse and finally died and was cremated.

Married Life Grows Worse

Up to this point, I had been through so much in my life, and still I had to face more pain.

I started back to work, and now I had two children, which made things even harder for me. Living with an abusive husband was the worst situation I had ever had to deal with.

Some people might ask, "Why would you stay with someone like that?" I wanted more than anything for my marriage to work. I kept praying and believing, and he only got worse.

The church I attended prayed and fasted for me. I fasted, prayed, and cried, and nothing changed. As I stated earlier, I did not realize that God would not go against Tyrone's will. As with all of us, God wanted Tyrone to come to Him of his own free will, not as a result of being forced to do someone else's will. God does not create us as robots. He gives us a free will, so that when we choose Him, it is a free choice, not something that is forced upon us and something that is done grudgingly.

I finally ended up leaving, staying with my brother in Pennsylvania for a while and then moving into a vacant trailer that my brother owned. I enjoyed the peace of not having to argue. I was no longer gripped with the fear of being beaten. My kids seemed happier, and things were going well.

My husband kept calling, crying, and begging me to come back. He promised me the world, and I fell for it. He said he had changed.

Little did I realize that it was just a ploy to get me back to New York.

I was deceived and walked back into the same situation. In fact, things rapidly grew much worse. God has since given me a platform to talk with women all over the world. As a result of my experience, I tell victims of abuse to never stay in an abusive relationship. They need to get themselves and their children to a safe place.

It was not God's original intent that His children should suffer abuse; however, we live in a fallen world, and abuse is rampant throughout this dark earthly realm.

I have had friends who were murdered by an abusive spouse or partner that they stayed with for too long. A man is supposed to love his wife, as God loves the church, His bride, and gave His life for her.

> *Husbands, love your wives, even as Christ also loved the church, and gave himself for it.*
>
> *(Ephesians 5:25)*

The Lord said that when a man mistreats his wife, he mistreats his own body, because they are one.

So ought men to love their wives as their own bodies. He that loveth his wife loveth himself. For no man ever yet hated his own flesh; but nourisheth and cherisheth it, even as the Lord the church.

(*Ephesians 5:28-29*)

My husband and I seemed to get along for a short time, then suddenly the abuse escalated. I never knew what would set him off. He could only go for brief periods without arguing. If I tried to defend myself, he grew even more upset. I was in a no-win situation.

I felt some relief from Tyrone's abuse when I went to work. I loved my job with the telephone company. It was so wonderful working there. They treated their employees very well and paid well, also. The management even allowed us to use one of their conference rooms to conduct Bible studies.

During one Bible study, while we were praying, my husband burst through the door and came straight for me. One of the men in the group stood in front of me so that Tyrone could not hit me. They began fighting, and the police came and took my husband out of the building in handcuffs. I was so humiliated that this all happened in front of my boss and coworkers.

It was a very trying time for me. I did not know what to do. I lived in paralyzing fear daily. My oldest daughter, at six years old, was so nervous, her grades suddenly began to drop in school. In addition, poor April

> PARALYZING
> FEAR

began to experience constant pain in her stomach because of the stress. Consequently, the school called me to come in for a meeting. They wanted to talk to me about April.

The school informed me that they noticed something was terribly wrong with April and that she seemed very sad. I told them about what was taking place in our home. They told me that I had to do something about it, or they would call youth services.

I was beside myself. I didn't know what to do. I knew I couldn't stay in New York, because Tyrone would never leave me alone; however, I did not want to lose my home and break up my family.

I rationalized that Tyrone had never hit the kids. He seemed to treat them well. He even taught April how to roller skate and ice skate. He bought her anything she wanted. We even went to Disney World as a family, and that was very exciting!

But Tyrone still had a very abusive nature, and I unfortunately had to bear the brunt of his abuse. If I had not had a relationship with God, I would have had a nervous breakdown. I read the Bible constantly, and that is where I received my strength. I also watched Christian television frequently.

God's mercy was new every day for me. He was my refuge and strength, and a very present help in time of trouble.

God is our refuge and strength, a very present help in trouble. Therefore will not we fear, though the earth be removed, and though the mountains be carried into the midst of the sea.

(Psalm 46:1-2)

On my way home from work one day, I felt that something was wrong. I went through the front door, and my husband was yelling at April about the math homework she was attempting to do. She was crying, and I told Tyrone to stop. He just called me stupid. April was ten years old at the time.

In the midst of Tyrone's onslaught of verbal abuse, I finally got April away from him. I picked my youngest daughter off the floor and told my husband I was going to the video store. I got in the car with both my daughters and drove to a friend's house. I knew I could not go back.

THE POINT OF NO RETURN

Tyrone came looking for me and found me. He began pounding on my friend's door and upsetting everyone in the house. My friend told me that I had to leave, because my husband was scaring her children. I did not know what to do.

I didn't dare return to what had become a house of horrors. I had to find safety.

I remembered a friend of mine who lived in Brooklyn, and I called her. She and her husband told me I was welcome in their home. I knew Tyrone could not follow me there, because I had never mentioned them to him. He didn't know where they lived. Under cover of night, I drove to Brooklyn. My children and I arrived safely and had a good night's sleep.

I got up the next morning and went to court to get an order of protection. There were many other women there for the same reason. I was granted the papers I needed to get Tyrone out of the house.

I went back home, and this time I took the police with me. They made Tyrone leave. He argued the whole time, but he had to leave. I remember it being so peaceful without him there. It was wonderful. But Tyrone's words haunted me when he had coldly declared years earlier, "If someone wants to kill you, an order of protection won't stop them."

I began to make plans to move back to Pennsylvania. I had to put distance between myself and Tyrone. I had to get to a safe place.

I had to go back to court to get permission to take my daughters out of the state of New York. The law in New York states that a woman can only take her children a certain distance away from the father, which for me was New Jersey.

Counselors at an abuse center told me to take the kids and just leave. They told me that I would stand a better chance of getting to Pennsylvania if I just left without going to court. But I could not do that. God told me not to fear the courts and that He was with me, and it would be all right.

And when they bring you unto the synagogues, and unto magistrates, and powers, take ye no thought how or what thing ye shall answer, or what ye shall say: For the Holy Spirit shall teach you in the same hour what ye ought to say.
(Luke 12:11-12)

God told me that He would part the Red Sea for me, if I trusted Him.

I hired a woman to come to the house to watch my daughters. Little did I know that she was a Christian. I told her I was going to court and explained to her the reason, and she prayed for me and prophesied over my life and confirmed to me what God had already told me.

God said in His Word that He goes ahead of us and makes our crooked way straight. He makes a way out of no way.

I will go before thee, and make the crooked places straight: I will break in pieces the gates of brass, and cut in sunder the bars of iron.

(Isaiah 45:2)

When I went to court, God made the crooked places straight, broke down the gates of brass, and cut through the bars of iron. My husband was there with his lawyer, and his lawyer tried to make me look unstable, but God was with me.

In spite of my husband telling the judge that I was stupid and did not know what I was talking about, God protected me. God says in His Word that He holds the king's heart in His hand, and He turns it whichever way He wants.

The king's heart is in the hand of the LORD, as the rivers of water: he turneth it whithersoever he will.

(Proverbs 21:1)

True to His Word, God gave me favor with the judge. My husband started shouting at the judge, and the judge told him to shut up. The judge asked me what I wanted the court to do for me. He declared that he would do whatever I said. I told him that I wanted to move to Pennsylvania, because I had family there. The judge granted my petition. God is forever faithful!

For the LORD is good; his mercy is everlasting; and his truth endureth to all generations.

(Psalm 100:5)

Chapter Five

Free at Last!

I left my husband, the house, and my car. In fact, the only possessions I took were clothes for me and my daughters. I resigned from my job at the telephone company, where I had been an employee for 23 years. God told me that wherever He led me, He would provide.

> *But my God shall supply all your need according to his riches in glory by Christ Jesus.*
>
> *(Philippians 4:19)*

The telephone company paid all of the transportation costs we incurred to travel to Pennsylvania. I moved in with my grandmother, and then eventually moved back into the trailer my brother let me use when I left my husband previously.

It was wonderful living next door to my grandmother. She was such a blessing to me and my children. God blessed my daughters to be able to spend time with their grandmother before she passed away. It was wonderful to be around my grandmother, hearing her pray and experiencing her ministry to me and my kids.

The trailer we lived in had three bedrooms and a big yard, where deer came to graze in the evening. It was a beautiful environment. Even though we lived in a very modest home, my daughters and I enjoyed rest and peace, at last.

> *And the peace of God, which passeth all understanding, shall keep your hearts and minds through Christ Jesus.*
> *(Philippians 4:7)*

Because we lived in a rural setting, when we went outside we had to make sure we did not step on any snakes. I have to say, though, it was a small price to pay for the wonderful peace we enjoyed. To this day, I thank God every single day of my life that I have peace in my home.

My mother's best friend lived in the home behind us and became the kids' godmother. She was very nice and was a great help to me in raising my children.

I began putting my life back together again with God's help. I was so happy to be living in an atmosphere of peace. Since I had given up my job when we moved to Pennsylvania, I began looking for work. Unfortunately, I could not find a job in the area where I lived. The economy was very slow, and there were no job openings.

I had to go on public assistance, which I did not want to do. My entire adult life, I had always worked, and now I had to be on welfare, and I hated it. After making $50,000 a year, here I was with food

TRUST GOD

stamps. I cried out to God, and He said, "Trust me. Wherever I lead you, I will provide." I replied, "Okay, God. I trust you."

Soon after, I received an unexpected call from the New York Telephone Company. They told me they were going to retire me with a pension and medical benefits. I could not believe it. I even asked, "Do you have the right Barbara Shaw?" I reminded them I was only 40 years old. I did not have the age nor length of service requirements to retire.

They laughed and told me they had the right person. They gave me a pension and a benefits package. They also sent me a 19-inch color television; plus, I received free local telephone service.

God is faithful if we trust Him. All things are possible to those who believe.

> *Jesus said unto him, If thou canst believe, all things are possible to him that believeth.*
>
> *(Mark 9:23)*

> *For with God nothing shall be impossible.*
>
> *(Luke 1:37)*

God proved to me again that He is able to do so much more than we can ever ask or imagine.

Now unto him that is able to do exceeding abundantly above all that we ask or think, according to the power that worketh in us, unto him be glory in the church by Christ Jesus throughout all ages, world without end. Amen.
(Ephesians 3:20-21)

Here I was, resigned from the telephone company. God was with me, so who could be against me?

What shall we say to these things? If God be for us, who can be against us?
(Romans 8:31)

I am destined by God for His excellent purpose and so are my children.

And again, I will put my trust in him. And again, Behold I and the children which God hath given me.
(Hebrews 2:13)

Behold, I and the children whom the LORD hath given me are for signs and for wonders in Israel from the LORD of hosts, which dwelleth in mount Zion.

(Isaiah 8:18)

God is so faithful. I was retired at 40 years of age, with benefits for me and my children. Praise God!!!

An Introduction to Ministry

While shopping one day, I ran into Lindsey Jones, a friend who had attended the same high school I had. She was married to another friend of mine, Victor Jones. She invited me to their church, where they both pastored.

While attending the Jones' church, I grew in the Lord. Lindsey prophesied over me and told me I was a mighty woman of God. She declared, "You are called to preach." I answered, "I can't speak in front of people." She replied, "You will."

Little did Lindsey know that I was already aware that God was calling me to a higher purpose, even though I still didn't comprehend its scope. One Saturday out of each month, the church had services for

CALLED
TO
PREACH

women, and I was asked to preach at one of those services.

I told Lindsey that I could not get up in front of those women and speak. She looked me right in the eye and told me again that I was a mighty woman of God, and she knew that God had a lot in me, and the women needed to hear what God wanted to say through me. Lindsey told me that I was going to preach.

When the time came, I got up and opened my mouth, and the Holy Spirit took over. It was wonderful. I loved it. God anointed me to minister to people and see their lives change. I loved being God's vessel of honor instead of the vessel of dishonor I had been in the past.

Sins of the Flesh

An old boyfriend called me, my very first boyfriend, and I had always had a soft place for him in my heart. But I thought that I was surely over him now. After all, I was more spiritually mature, now that I was in my 40s.

When I heard Mitch's voice, it was like I went into a trance and could not resist him. I let him come to see me and my kids. The next thing I knew, I was caught up in fornication, illicit sex. To make things even worse, he was married, so I was again committing adultery.

The whole time I was involved in this affair, I was under the conviction of the Holy Spirit. The peace God had given me was now gone. I could not sleep. I cried out to God Almighty to deliver me. The conviction was so strong, that I would break off with Mitch, but then fall to temptation and let him back in my life over and over again.

HOLY SPIRIT CONVICTION

God told me very clearly that He had not delivered me from an abusive husband just to have me run to another man. He delivered me so that I could run to Him! God also told me that He was giving me enough time to make it right and break off the relationship; but if I did not, He was going to do it, and that I would not like the way He did it.

Of course, that frightened me, because I know God does not lie, and He means what He says.

> *God is not a man, that he should lie; neither the son of man, that he should repent: hath he said, and shall he not do it? or hath he spoken, and shall he not make it good?*
> *(Numbers 23:19)*

God is a jealous God, and He does not want us to place anything above Him.

> *For thou shalt worship no other god: for the LORD, whose name is Jealous, is a jealous God.*
> *(Exodus 34:14)*

I lamented over the affair for the next couple of months. I told Mitch that I was miserable, because my life belonged to God, and I could not continue the affair. Mitch was not saved, so he didn't understand my change of heart.

He did not take me seriously, because I had broken off the affair with him before and did not stick to my word. So, even though I told him I did not want to see him again, he came back the next day. This time, however, it was different, because I was different.

> *Therefore if any man be in Christ, he is a new creature: old things are passed away; behold, all things are become new.*
>
> *(2 Corinthians 5:17)*

I felt the Holy Spirit rise up inside me, and I told Mitch to get out and not come back. I did not see him again after that. I am so grateful to God for His mercy, His patience with me, and for His love. God delivered me and set me free again! His love never fails!

Thy mercy, O L<small>ORD</small>, is in the heavens; and thy faithfulness reacheth unto the clouds. Thy righteousness is like the great mountains; thy judgments are a great deep: O L<small>ORD</small>, thou preservest man and beast. How excellent is thy lovingkindness, O God! therefore the children of men put their trust under the shadow of thy wings.

(Psalm 36:5-7)

The Battle Rages

In the months to come, my brother had a serious heart attack; my grandmother died in her sleep, and I found her in her bed; then my youngest daughter, Renee, got very sick in school, and the school did not inform me. When she finally got home, she fell in the door. I rushed her to the emergency room, and they told me she had scarlet fever.

I was under so much stress that I had to go to a doctor for my nerves. I was prescribed one

> NOTHING SEEMED TO WORK

antidepressant after another, and I had a grocery bag full of medication. Nothing seemed to work. Even though I listened to Christian radio and watched Christian television every day, I still felt a heavy burden.

Victory!

Suddenly, seemingly out of nowhere, God delivered me Himself without any medication. My hair had fallen out, but it grew back. God is so awesome! Even though we will surely have tribulation, Jesus is the answer to every problem we will ever face.

These things I have spoken unto you, that in me ye might have peace. In the world ye shall have tribulation: but be of good cheer; I have overcome the world.
(Exodus 34:14)

God told me that I would not die, but live and declare His works (Psalm 118:17). And that's exactly what I do. I declare His works. My life is not my own. I have been bought with the price of Jesus' blood.

> *For ye are bought with a price: therefore glorify God in your body, and in your spirit, which are God's.*
> *(1 Corinthians 6:20)*

I now walk by faith and not by sight!

> *(For we walk by faith, not by sight:)*
> *(2 Corinthians 5:7)*

After all I have been through, I now realize that God has always been faithful. It is such a pleasure and an honor to serve the One who died for me. It seems such a small sacrifice, to totally give Him my life; after all, He gave me His.

What I have to look forward to now is constant blessing and increase for me and my daughters. I am filled with hope that I will now live a life filled with victory!

Chapter Six
Life in Christ

I am so happy to finally be free! It's like a dream, but it's very real. God called me to attend World Harvest Church in Columbus, Ohio, and God has given me and my daughters a life that I could not have dreamed was possible.

If the Son therefore shall make you free, ye shall be free indeed.

(John 8:36)

I am in awe of my surroundings, to be free at last and to see the world from a new perspective. I have a greater appreciation of life because of what I have been through. God has given me a new spiritual outlook, and He has changed everything in my life!

Life is so wonderful, and God is so awesome. What I have been through has made me stronger. As I look at my daughters, who are adults now, I know they won't go through what I've been through. I've passed on to them what I've learned. I believe God has given them wisdom, so they will not walk down the same path of sorrow and abuse that I did.

Tyrone and I live in separate states. I have forgiven him and moved on with my life. He calls me and our daughters occasionally to check on us and to let us know how he is doing. Although our daughters do not have a close relationship with their father, he sometimes provides financial support if they need it, for which I am grateful.

Children's lives are shaped and molded by what they experience. As believers, we have to back up what we say by how we live our lives. God has strengthened my daughters and blessed them, even in adversity. (Or I should say He has blessed them <u>especially</u> in adversity.)

God makes everything new if we let Him. I can walk into the future knowing the old has passed away, and everything is brand new in my life and in the lives of my children. We are free!

My story is not unique; this is the story of many others. I am only one of millions who have been horribly abused by their mate. "On average, nearly 20 people per minute are physically abused by an intimate partner in the United States. During one year, this equates to more than 10 million women and men. 1 in 3 women and 1 in 4 men have been victims of [some form of] physical violence by an intimate partner within their lifetime."[3]

> MY STORY IS NOT UNIQUE

It is a nightmare many face: the person that was supposed to love you is your worst enemy. Even though I cried out for help from family, friends, and even the church, no one listened. They believed it was not as bad as I said. Some even told me not to leave my abuser.

---

[3] ncadv.org/learn-more/statistics

God never meant for any of us to be abused by anyone, especially those who are supposed to love and cherish us. Do not be a statistic. Take whatever precautions you have to take to live in a safe environment. We have laws designed to help and protect us. Utilize those laws. Protect yourself and your children.

May the Lord awaken you in the morning with His voice and may you lie down in the evening trusting Him. May the Lord bless you indeed, enlarge your territory, and may His hand be with you and keep you from evil, that you will not be grieved. God bless you!

And Jabez called on the God of Israel, saying, Oh that thou wouldest bless me indeed, and enlarge my coast, and that thine hand might be with me, and that thou wouldest keep me from evil, that it may not grieve me! And God granted him that which he requested.
(1 Chronicles 4:10)

Chapter Seven
An Invitation

I am so glad that I had a chance to accept Jesus Christ as my Savior. There are so many of my friends and relatives that had a chance to accept Him in their lives, but did not. They thought they had plenty of time to come to Him later in their lives.

God said in His Word:

Wherefore (as the Holy Spirit saith, To day if ye will hear his voice, harden not your hearts, as in the provocation, in the day of temptation in the wilderness...)
(Hebrews 3:7-8)

Tomorrow is promised to no man. Those friends and relatives of mine who, as far as I know, never accepted Christ, died the way they lived – apart from God. They wanted nothing to do with Jesus. If they did not accept Him as Savior before they passed away, they will have to spend eternity in hell, forever separated from Him. I pray that they made the right choice before they entered eternity.

Those of you reading this book who have not accepted Jesus Christ as your personal Savior and the Lord of your life, I am presenting to you an opportunity to accept the greatest gift you could ever receive: eternal life in paradise with God. Jesus is the only way to God! He is the Way, the Truth, and the Life. No man comes to the Father except through Jesus.

Jesus saith unto him, I am the way, the truth, and the life: no man cometh unto the Father, but by me.

(John 14:6)

Jesus is the door to eternal life in the Kingdom of God.

> *Then said Jesus unto them again, Verily,*
> *verily, I say unto you, I am the door of*
> *the sheep ... I am the door: by me if any*
> *man enter in, he shall be saved, and shall*
> *go in and out, and find pasture.*
> *(John 10:7, 9)*

I pray that my testimony will help you make wise choices. I made disastrous decisions that negatively impacted my life. You can make the right decision today to give your life to Jesus; and I promise you, your life will never be the same. Choose today whom you will serve. You must serve God or Satan. There is no in between. Choose life.

> *I call heaven and earth to record this day*
> *against you, that I have set before you*
> *life and death, blessing and cursing:*
> *therefore choose life, that both thou and*
> *thy seed may live...*
> *(Deuteronomy 30:19)*

> *And if it seem evil unto you to serve the*
> *LORD, choose you this day whom ye will*

serve; whether the gods which your fathers served that were on the other side of the flood, or the gods of the Amorites, in whose land ye dwell: but as for me and my house, we will serve the LORD.

(Joshua 24:15)

The gift of God is eternal life through Jesus Christ. If you would like to choose eternal life in paradise with Christ, repeat this prayer:

Lord Jesus Christ, I come to you today, knowing I was born a sinner. I ask you to forgive me of my sins. Satan, I renounce you and will not serve you. Go from me now. Lord Jesus Christ, I accept you as my Savior and Lord. I believe in you and will serve you as you show me how. Fill me with your Holy Spirit to lead me in your ways, and I will serve you all the days of my life. Amen.

You Have Victory!

Congratulations! You are now a part of the family of God and destined for victory in Christ Jesus! Read your Bible daily. It is the inerrant Word of God that will give you instruction for every situation you will ever face in this life. Find a church

> VICTORY
> IN JESUS!

that preaches the Word of God and is filled with His Holy Spirit. Witness to others about the new life you have found through Jesus Christ.

Finally, always take time to pray. It is your way to communicate with God.

Pray without ceasing.
(1 Thessalonians 5:17)

Prayer is not a religious ritual that requires you to repeat prideful, ineffective, unproductive words.

But when ye pray, use not vain repetitions, as the heathen do: for they think that they shall be heard for their much speaking. Be not ye therefore like

Bar

unto them: for your Father knoweth what things ye have need of, before ye ask him. After this manner therefore pray ye: Our Father which art in heaven, Hallowed be thy name. Thy kingdom come, Thy will be done in earth, as it is in heaven. Give us this day our daily bread. And forgive us our debts, as we forgive our debtors. And lead us not into temptation, but deliver us from evil: For thine is the kingdom, and the power, and the glory, for ever. Amen.

(Matthew 6:7-13)

Prayer is simply communicating with God. Talk to Him, and He will hear and answer your prayers.

Call unto me, and I will answer thee, and show thee great and mighty things, which thou knowest not.

(Jeremiah 33:3)

Even more importantly, listen for God's voice and follow His guidance, no matter what. His direction will <u>always</u> lead you to follow the path of His love, which is grounded in truth, the Word of God. Talk to Him as you would a dear friend, because He is the best friend you will ever have. He is a friend that sticks closer than a brother.

> *...there is a friend that sticketh closer than a brother.*
>
> *(Proverbs 18:24b)*

I pray for you now, that you will clearly hear God's voice within you and become victorious in every area of your life through the mighty power of God's Holy Spirit, who dwells within you. You, too, are destined by God!

www.ingramcontent.com/pod-product-compliance
Lightning Source LLC
Chambersburg PA
CBHW060358050426
42449CB00009B/1796